T0128696

SACRED VERSES

PART THREE
(THE JOURNEY OF THE SPIRIT)

GENE JACKSON

iUniverse, Inc.
Bloomington

SACRED VERSES
PART THREE, THE JOURNEY OF THE SPIRIT

The views expressed in this work are solely those of the author and do not necessarily reflect the views of the publisher, and the publisher hereby disclaims any responsibility for them.

iUniverse books may be ordered through booksellers or by contacting:

iUniverse
1663 Liberty Drive
Bloomington, IN 47403
www.iuniverse.com
1-800-Authors (1-800-288-4677)

Because of the dynamic nature of the Internet, any web addresses or links contained in this book may have changed since publication and may no longer be valid.

Any people depicted in stock imagery provided by Thinkstock are models, and such images are being used for illustrative purposes only.

Certain stock imagery © Thinkstock.

ISBN: 978-1-4697-7189-2 (sc)
ISBN: 978-1-4697-7190-8 (e)

Printed in the United States of America

iUniverse rev. date: 03/08/2012

To Chris:

". . .for he was like, had he been tried,

to have proved most royal."

and, To David,

the Spartan.

AUTHOR'S NOTE

The *Divine Comedy* of Dante Alighieri was written in a strict rhyme scheme of *Terza Rima*. This is possible in Italian, but not in English and therefore all of these verses are in sonnet form. By far, the majority are Italian (or Petrarchian), but each chapter ends in one or more Shakespearean sonnets. This is, as far as I am aware, the longest sonnet sequence in English literature. The verses are described as *Sacred,* not in the sense of *Holy* or *Devout* but in the classical or medieval sense of relating to the spiritual or intellectual universe, instead of the body and physical world, which would be *Profane.*

In the first volume the young man has sought an overview of the physical world, which corresponds to the *Inferno* of Dante. The second volume is concerned with philosophy or an intellectual attempt to understand the universe and would be considered a parallel to the *Purgatorio* of Dante. This third volume and the fourth (yet to come) will examine the spiritual aspects of our world and may be regarded as a counterpart to Dante's *Paradisio.*

"Only to gods in heaven
    Comes no old age or death of anything.
      All else is turmoiled by our master, Time.
        Earth's glory fades,
          And mankind's strength will go away;
Faith dies, and Unfaith blossoms like a flower.
    And who can find, in the open streets of men
      Or secret places of his own heart's love
        One wind blow true forever?"

Sophocles

"Oedipus at Colonnae"

"But soon we too shall die,
    And all memory of those we loved will have left the earth,
      And we ourselves shall be loved for a while and then forgotten.
But the love will have been enough;
    All those impulses of love return to the love that made them.
Even memory is not necessary for love;

There is a land of the living and a land of the dead,
    And the bridge is love,
      The only survival,
        The only meaning."

T. Wilder

"The Bridge of San Luis Rey"

VOLUME THREE

THE JOURNEY OF THE SPIRIT

Humility and Grace
    Mother Teresa 1

The Old Master
    Lao Tze 9

The Great Teacher
    Confucius 31

The Enlightened One
    the Buddha 55

The Patriarch
    Isaiah 75

HUMILITY AND GRACE

Because I knew that I had not yet gained
The understanding that for years I sought,
Despite my teachers, even though they taught
Philosophy and science that contained
Much truthfulness, yet something else remained
Beyond the realm of proof or human thought.
My destiny already had been wrought,
Completion of my journey pre-ordained;
As if, called forth from mystical seclusion,
Appearing as a whirling cloud of sand
From eastern deserts, some immortal djinn,
Possessed and angry as a wild illusion,
Had judged my prior expeditions and
Condemned me to repeat them once again.

The chains of memory, once forged, will last;
Unbroken, they will never disappear,
Constraining us, although we persevere,
So we are bound forever to our past.
Our future pathways cannot be forecast,
For even though our search may be sincere,
The space ahead of us, our life's frontier,
Is ill-defined, ambiguous, and vast.
And yet we try, attempting to resolve
The central quandary of our existence:
How should we live, so that our lives might show
The growth inherent as our souls evolve,
And demonstrate a virtuous consistence
Profound as any we could ever know.

Although I recognized where I began
So long ago, I was again alone
Within the tangled wilderness I'd known.
Then (as before), a sign, a talisman
Appeared, and this a tired pedestrian
Accepted gladly, partly to atone
For needing even more than I'd been shown;
It offered me a third and final plan.
If I would file away what I had learned,
Accepting as correct but incomplete
My knowledge of the world, then I might enter
Another plane I had 'til now discerned
But dimly; here I must once more repeat
My search, but once again I'd have a mentor.

On reading this, I slowly looked around,
To see what guiding image might be waiting.
For at this point, I was anticipating
A shining saintly figure, with profound
Authority, and certainly renowned
Religiosity, and radiating
Divine delight, instead of contemplating
A tiny person, sitting on the ground.
It was a woman, formless, indistinct,
And fitted with a strange accoutrement.
Her voice was almost harsh, direct, with few
Refinements, with an accent, but succinct
Significance; it came as from a tent,
For she was draped in cloth of white and blue.

She spoke to me, not as a prophet speaks
With bombast, gestures and exaggeration,
Or attitude that borders affectation,
Or metaphors or eloquent techniques.
She had no secret or occult mystiques
To show an esoteric connotation;
There was no hidden or obscure causation
But only guidance, as a pilgrim seeks.
She spoke directly, simply, honestly,
And seemed to know the reason I was there,
As if she had been watching all the while
That I had wandered through antiquity,
Despite my efforts finding everywhere
Enigmas that I could not reconcile.

"You will be welcome here, but I must say,
You seem much older than I thought you'd be.
Perhaps one's youth is just illusory,
A thin veneer that simply falls away,
Revealing inner features which outweigh
Apparent confidence and certainty;
These will give way to vague anxiety
Whenever life appears in disarray.
So, you have traveled many miles to gain
Discernment of the world and of ideas,
And many learned doctors clarified
That part of truth that lay in their domain.
Have you discovered any panaceas?
With all your learning, are you satisfied?"

"And have you let your mind betray your soul?
For knowledge is a fickle mistress yet,
It will not comfort you in time of threat,
And when you are distressed, will not console.
For you have learned a part, but not the whole
Of universal life, do not forget
That there is no protective amulet
That will in chaos keep you in control.
You have not yet determined how to live
In this immensely complicated world
In which existence cannot be abstraction.
And so to live, it is imperative
That you be stable, never spun or whirled,
And learn serenity and satisfaction."

"So I must ask you once again to go
And seek enlightenment, a different kind;
Leave science and philosophy behind,
Progress into a spiritual plateau,
And you will find tranquility, although
The pathway there may not be well-defined,
Since many canons need to be combined
Into a viable scenario.
And though in life there is no final test,
The price of unawareness is severe:
Existence in a black and empty hole.
Pure science shows the cosmos manifest,
The intellect will teach you what to fear;
Salvation is created in the soul."

"But so that you will not come back confused,
I need to give directions and advice:
Do not solicit keys to paradise,
That term itself is frequently misused;
The very concept often is abused
By charlatans, those hoping to entice
The lost, who cannot make the sacrifice
Of easy opportunity, refused.
For true enlightenment is always earned,
And unlike science, it cannot be proved,
In contrast to philosophy, its logic
May not be always easily discerned.
Beware the ecstasy that leaves you moved,
For revelations can be demagogic."

"Beware the prophet claiming absolute
Inerrant truth from his own inspiration;
This may be theologic fabrication,
Especially if meant to persecute
The non-conforming skeptics who dispute
A rigid dogma with no deviation,
Or doctrine that promotes the condemnation
Of weakness, prodigals, the dissolute.
For love is positive, does not condemn,
And demonstrates no pride or arrogance,
But seeks to balance strong and weak, by reaching
Out to the fragile, elevating them.
By doing this it shows a radiance
More eloquent than any kind of preaching."

"But you will meet philosophers and priests,
Of secular or catholic theology,
Who claim their own inerrancy, at least,
And some of both maintain without apology
That ritual or dogma is essential
Before salvation is to be achieved;
And many other things are consequential
If complicated doctrines are believed.
But few can see, or teach the pure expression
Of charity, of giving all you can;
For love, experienced, becomes obsession
Far nobler than the strictest puritan.
For life is love, and you must live that way,
No matter what the priests or skeptics say."

Before I left, I asked her who had sent
Her to this place, who told her I would be
Along these winding roads, a refugee,
And how she knew my needs and my intent.
She represented the embodiment
Of moral certainty, and was the key,
Past all my prior learning, guiding me
Toward final, ultimate enlightenment.
But to my question, she could not respond;
She did not know, more likely not recall
The individuals, "We all are one,
In history, in this life and beyond,
As we have been together here, we all
Will meet again," she said, and then was gone.

But I had faith that she would reappear
At some far-off and destined place when my
Confusion was suppressed, my course made clear,
And all my life was open to the sky.
I still had far to go before I rested,
But she provided hope that I might finish
And justify the time I had invested;
Awareness would increase, and not diminish.
I had begun my journey unaware,
And though with time my insight was expanding
Enough to banish danger of despair,
I had not reached a final understanding.
But she had offered me one last dimension
That was, for now, beyond my comprehension.

THE OLD MASTER

Then on the level road, but far away,
I saw a plodding water buffalo
Approaching with a steady pace and slow,
And on his back, a man attired in gray.
Their pace was sensible, without delay
But also without needless haste, as though
Extended journeys, planned so long ago
Required a firm intent, no disarray.
He was alone, appearing to prefer
His solitude, for that way he could ride
Without a crowd or any human links.
I sensed an unexpected character
And disconcerted, I was mystified:
A strange elusive creature, like a sphinx.

He seemed a simple man who, long ago,
Had solved the problem of the disarray
Our lives beget. I asked him to survey
His understanding, wisdom it would show,
But his response was reticent, although
He said this to his would-be protégé:
That those who know the secrets do not say,
And those who give an answer do not know.
He seemed indifferent, not impolite,
Preferring privacy to fellowship;
And since his height would let him overlook
An ignorant apprentice acolyte,
He then, before continuing his trip
Reached down and handed me a slender book.

The noble Master's magnetism lay
Within a sense that seemed to indicate
That he possessed a depth, an ultimate
Insight to life, its growth and its decay.
But he proceeded, disinclined to stay
Or socialize or teach or even wait
Until I had the time to contemplate
What secrets his appearance might convey.
For his ungainly mount set off again,
Along a gentle rise and toward the crest;
I followed him as far as I could look
Into the farthest distance, only then
When he had disappeared into the west,
I sat upon the ground and read his book.

The volume in itself was very thin,
The time required to read it, moderate;
I finished it in half an hour, yet
I felt I still was ready to begin.
My grasp of all the principles within
Was incomplete, but I could not forget
The strange and mystic figure; with regret
I still recalled the ancient mandarin,
The recluse who, absorbed in meditation
Had sought a further, secret solitude,
Retiring somewhere, even to Tibet,
And set out for that distant destination.
His path, unplanned, had circled to include
This very site, the point at which we met.

His book, transcendent in its central thought,
Involved the concept of the *path,* or *way*;
But written words or speech can not convey
Nor mind conceive the essence that it sought.
The meanings of the images it brought
Were vast, beyond the strength of words to say
Or minds to comprehend, their value lay
Beyond the ordered reason we are taught.
They touched an ultimate reality,
The mystic *path,* the never-ending *way*
That leads us from the source of life and springs
From centers and beginnings that we see
Unclearly even in the light of day,
And not at all through nights and evenings.

The *pathway* emanates out of the Womb
Of all of life and of the universe;
From unity its essence will disperse
As light from central candles fills a room,
Illuminating beings, all of whom
Surrounded by this entity immerse
Their senses in these secrets and rehearse
Responses to the wonder they consume.
But equally, creation flowing out
Returns unto the place where it began,
And thus eternal cycles are resolved.
How certain and coherent, all devout
Observers see this mode as greater than
Contrasting images which have evolved.

This principle is also *immanent,*
The course by which all life must operate;
The driving force of nature, consummate
In order and a dominant intent
That moves the universe, but ambient,
Participates in life, renewing great
And minor rhythms, and will animate
The living world and all the firmament.
It cannot be exhausted, for it flows
According to demand; and never dry,
It is the fountain that is always on.
Benign and graceful, still it spares no rose
Because of beauty, nor the butterfly,
For each will live awhile, and then be gone.

Another sense of *pathway* or the *Tao*
Refers to human life, which must align
With universal passages, combine
With other essences, for these endow
Our lives with higher meaning and allow
Expansion past the fixed, confining line
That limits our capacity, the fine
Distinction of *supreme* from *here-and-now*.
To *be* something, to *know* something, to *rise*
Above the undistinguished superficial,
Gives life a higher substance, they access
The mystic wisdom and the magic prize
That no one dreamed when they began initial
Endeavors to escape their mindlessness.

To journey on this path relies on *power*,
Upon the infinitely generous
And integrating spirit, luminous
And orderly, our law and arbiter.
Because it flows with purpose through each hour
Of all our lives, providing impetus,
We must not spend it on mere frivolous
Irrelevance, a vain malingerer.
We must increase, at least conserve the force,
To live both wisely and efficiently,
Creating lives of pure effectiveness.
So we must interrupt, close to the source
Whatever drains our vital energy,
Eliminating friction and distress.

There have been some who said this strength is stable,
And fixed for all the time we are alive,
Thus one can not enhance (but can deprive)
Himself of means that often will enable
Each person to achieve all he is able;
This means to know himself and so to thrive,
Within a world of chaos, to survive
Avoiding all the furies that disable.
For those who feel this potency is fixed,
Preserving it is foremost; conservation
Means first, expending it efficiently.
Thus knowledge must be pure and never mixed;
The form enhancing life, self-preservation,
Is *wisdom,* to be spent judiciously.

Each life should be a pattern that is wise,
Conserving its vitality, serene,
Avoiding useless acts that contravene
The balance and the peace that are the prize.
To drain one's energy will paralyze
Progression to the ultimate, the clean
And pure transcendent *way;* while in between
We stay in limbo, and we agonize.
The enemy is conflict and the friction
That comes with selfish striving and desire,
Ambition, discord, egotistic greed
And all the factors leading to constriction
Of useful energy that we aquire
Into a narrow corridor of need.

Contented souls are those who live in peace,
Surrounded by a pure tranquility,
Not interrupted by ill-feeling, free
Of frivolous ambivalence, caprice.
So when, by meditation we release
Our inhibitions, vital energy
Will flow throughout our being silently;
Vitality and vigor will increase.
This force, this energy in life is good,
To be more animated even better,
To be alive forever is the best.
But there are others who have understood
Awareness and acceptance like a debtor
Who must repay a loan with interest.

The opportunity might well exist
To multiply instead of just protect
Resources; inner powers may affect
Our present state as by a catalyst.
These hidden springs of consciousness consist
Of secret sources of the intellect
And of the soul, and these will intersect
To form the world of the idealist.
Good servants may increase their master's wealth
When trusted with a certain fixed amount,
Instead of hiding it within the ground
And then returning it with guilty stealth
In order to conceal the true account,
While sensing that their failure is profound.

Their talents, put to work at interest
Compound themselves, creating greater gain,
And efforts such as these are not in vain,
The servant has perceived and passed the test.
The master will be glad, the manifest
Enlargement of his assets will attain
The wherewithal to furnish his domain
To please himself, his servant and his guest.
And thus, resources in the human soul
May be increased, creating higher planes
Of affirmation and vitality.
There are some factors we cannot control,
But some we can; the best of these contains
The secret to achieving synergy.

To reach this space where all becomes serene
Requires sincere and earnest preparation;
Before commencing any meditation
The body, mind, and soul must all be clean.
The discipline of formalized routine
(The stretching and the postures, activation
Of physical awareness, concentration
On actionless activity), is keen.
Unique is one who "purified and swept"
Is free from all emotion, all desire,
Revulsion, grief, annoyance or delight;
For only peace and stillness can accept
Pure consciousness, the essence, holy fire,
Appearing as a beacon in the night.

When fear and all anxiety are quelled,
The cosmic harmony will come unsought
Into the mind, without a conscious thought
But with a force that is unparalleled.
Intangible and never yet beheld,
Adjacent, it is felt but never caught,
Remote, surrounds us when we are distraught,
Then all is still, and dissonance dispelled.
The Way of Vital Spirit fills our frames,
It comes, but always is intangible,
It seems to go, and yet has not departed;
Unspoken, outside claims and counter claims,
It overcomes each earthly obstacle
To re-enforce the spirit grown faint-hearted.

The purpose of our life is to align
Our essence with the boundless tide and flow
Of ultimate reality and show
How universal forms and ours combine;
As though we live along a waterline
And slip with quiet confidence below
The water's surface, trusting it although
We do not grasp its nature or design.
We know that if we struggle, thrash or flail
We surely will submerge ourselves and sink,
But when we gently breathe, relax and float
Upon the surface, then we will prevail.
So, understanding nature, we can link
Ourselves to confidence, as in a boat.

Observe a river, flowing quietly,
The water moving, never under strain
Across a miscellaneous terrain,
Its movement passive, drawn by gravity.
Its course seems effortless, but energy
Will move it forward past a level plain
And through impediments which might contain
Its even movement and consistency.
The stream ignores frontiers, flows under walls,
Reduces rocks and can erode a hill,
Adapts and searches without lethargy
The lowest places as its level falls.
It follows in its destined path until
Its journey closed, it merges with the sea.

Fast-moving streams above a rocky bed
Are clear and clean, transparent to the sight.
There one can see the pebbles, rounded, white,
And flashes from the many-faceted
Reflections of the objects overhead.
The schools of minnows flee and re-unite,
The rocks beneath the surface seem as bright
As if transparent air was there instead.
But when the current broadens, it will change,
Lethargic, sluggish, it becomes opaque,
And muddy sediment is now suspended
Within the water, giving it a strange
Unpleasant character, as if to make
A clouded channel, blurred and now distended.

A glass of water from this muddy pond
Initially appears as thick, unclear;
In time the sediment will disappear
And settle, vanish like a vagabond.
In grip of gravity, it will abscond,
Become a solid residue, adhere
To bottom surfaces, and you can peer
Through water cleansed, and see the world beyond.
This clarity will come into the mind
When life creates a quiet interlude
Allowing all distracting molecules
To fade away, and leaving these behind,
Achieves a comprehensive solitude
Resembling deep and reassuring pools.

The highest good, like water and the rain
That nourishes as if by accident,
Has no pretense or vanity, content
In lowly places all the rich disdain.
In order to participate, refrain
From violence and force and argument,
Be quietly effective, reticent,
Bombastic platitudes will be in vain.
But be like flowing water, quietly
Adapting to the hard and brittle places,
Diminishing and softening their edges.
Compliant as the river seems to be
Its destiny will follow empty spaces,
The tranquil stream erodes the rigid ledges.

The human quality that parallels
The river, always flowing free of stress
Is not an attitude of idleness
Abstaining vacantly like silent bells;
It is a quiet stirring which compels
Supreme activity, still effortless,
Effective but relaxed, without excess,
Attentive like a stronghold's sentinels.
The practice of creative quietude
Is flexible while still remaining pure,
Creating inner insights, comprehensions.
The moment inspiration is renewed
Is when the mind is vacant but secure,
Receptive to designs in new dimensions.

These principles of life are limitless
If we allow ourselves to intermix
Without resistance, as the candles' wicks
Allow the flame unlimited access.
And so it is that we must acquiesce
To bearing light, as do the candlesticks,
Achieve through silences, not rhetorics
A consummate and simple gracefulness.
No person lives a self-enclosed existence
As if he were an island, solitary,
Nor, as a whole, are humans self-contained;
We all require, and utilize assistance,
Collective energy is necessary
So loneliness and passion are restrained.

The essences of evil and of good
Are never diametric opposites;
They share a common tension that permits
A relativity if understood.
Polarity, dynamic balance should
Explain the prototype: that each one fits
Into the other, therefore neither quits
And neither overwhelms, although it could.
They occupy adjacent hemispheres
And circle cautiously, as in a dance
To take possession of the other's place,
Or be dispelled if something else appears.
Thus neither can achieve a dominance,
Both limited within their common space.

The value of a cup, a window, doors,
Lies in the parts of them that are not there;
The person touching them is not aware
Of usefulness the absent span restores.
We stand with firmness on the solid floors,
But when we climb, ascending on a stair,
We rise by faith into the empty air,
As confident as when an eagle soars.
This shows that what is more is often less,
And what we do not do says much of us;
Ambition, striving, are to no avail,
For competition always leads to stress.
To strive for victory is frivolous
And those who stretch to touch the stars will fail.

Conform to genuine and simple ways,
Befriend the world and do not dominate,
Attune yourself to nature, cultivate
The pattern and perfection it portrays.
Display an outward manner that conveys
Your inner deep respect, and demonstrate
Awareness of the beauties that await,
The symmetry that solitude displays.
The reasoning and convoluted rules,
The ceremonies and theology
That teachers, wise men, prophets justify
Are reassuring to the zealous fools
Who need compliance with formality,
The certainty that rituals imply.

We must assume that mysteries exist;
There is an essence, perfect, wonderful,
Created first, as by a miracle
Before the earth or mankind could assist.
How gentle and how clear the catalyst,
It is eternal, nothing can annul
The quiet, pure and supernatural,
The essence of the world's protagonist.
It stands alone and does not ever vary,
Will enter us as far as we allow;
It permeates the day, and also night,
In all its realm it has no adversary.
I do not know its name, but call it *Tao*,
The Way, and I can recognize its might.

In life and nature, seek the empty spaces;
There, move so lightly footprints do not show,
Your passage modest, so that none will know
That you have come and gone, and to what places.
Your life becomes a pleasing dance that traces
Simplicity and freedom that will flow
Without imbalance, an adagio
Expressing eloquent and flawless graces.
And speak so well your tongue can never slip,
Be eloquent, without an argument.
Express a logic, not an absolute,
And reason well beforehand, you may skip
Debate with those who are belligerent;
Persuade without a grandiose dispute.

The arrogant, who seek to dominate
The earth, and bend and shape it to their will
Have never yet prevailed, but they instill
A danger to the universe, inflate
Their own ambition, which they then equate
With benefit for all the world until
Profane destructive actions almost fill
Benign capacities to compensate.
The earth is like a holy sacred vessel
So delicate and pure that it is scarred
By careless conflict, grossly set upon.
The earth was meant to dance, they wish to wrestle,
The crude and coarse come near and it is marred,
And when they reach their fingers out, is gone.

There is no absolute polarity,
But varied cycles (like a pendulum),
That bend and join again and thus become
A balance and a tension, symmetry.
Thus good and evil, light and dark are free
To pass their opposite and overcome
The other, but in equilibrium;
Predominance is only cursory.
Distress and happiness are relative,
The summer and the winter alternate
And positive and negative attract;
Our active and our passive moods forgive
Each other constantly, we fluctuate
Between the forceful and the sheer abstract.

The progress in our lives is seldom straight
And never leads us upward to success;
The peaks and pinnacles toward which we press
Are out of reach and only aggravate.
Concentric limits all around create
An energy that bends us back, unless
We comprehend its nature, acquiesce,
And thus accept, conform, accommodate.
Each pair of values is resolved, enclosed
By one great circle with its limitation;
This boundary, eternally unbroken,
Can be approached, but never is opposed.
And life itself curves back in affirmation
Of ultimate reality, unspoken.

We sleep, and sometimes in this state we dream;
These fantasies are often sharp and clear,
But when we wake the visions disappear
Beyond recall, no matter what the theme.
Then we may wonder if the things that seem
To lie before us, lavish or austere
Express reality, and are we here
As mere illusions which we must redeem?
If you are tired, lie down and wake refreshed;
As sleep and wakefulness are cycles here
So life and death are complementary.
These interwoven entities are meshed,
When one is gone, the other will appear;
So rest, and sleep while dreaming peacefully.

.

The circles that surround us never cease,
But always turning inward, each re-traces
Its circuit to enclose protected spaces
Where all is one and all is well; release
Of spirits of support and their increase
Prevents ill-fated fortunes and disgraces,
Sustains us through the hard and hostile places
And then allows us to depart in peace.
The essence that had been our heritage,
When we were young and occupied with strife
Once gave us vigor, energy and breath,
But now provides serene and restful age.
The One who lent what we required in life
Will also give us what we need in death.

In life, the only final absolute
Is death, but this again is cyclical.
The change that brings us into being shall
Escort us out again and substitute
A fresher form for weary souls, transmute
Decrepit bodies into natural
But newer, rested states; perennial
Recycling is our greatest attribute.
And so, accept your status, reconcile
The disillusions of experience,
The failing strength of age, they are the norm.
When you are old, lie down and sleep awhile,
Despite distress, have faith and confidence;
The world is natural, and we conform.

The natural domain does not insist.
The sun may shine today, the rain may cease,
Or else, in half a day it could increase;
The two may alternate or co-exist,
Reality is never prejudiced,
Things happen as they will, as by caprice.
But if we are attuned, we may release
Vexation and become an optimist.
The common thread throughout the universe,
The basic principle that integrates
The whole of nature and of all our lives
Is vast vitality which will immerse
Receptive minds and spirits, and creates
A unity, the Way, which then survives.

The paradoxes of this world are such
As seem to violate our common sense,
The understated, subtle, rules the dense
And energy rules matter that we touch.
We reach for things we covet, try to clutch
Our heart's desire, but empty evidence
Reveals that it is gone, and abstinence
Enhances pain if we have loved too much.
Our consciousness commands our energy,
And wisdom can control our intuition,
Thus softness influences what is strong.
Our spirits must return to purity,
Denying all the lures of acquisition,
And finding what we needed all along.

The integrating principle is not
To be achieved by striving or through strain
And not by those who grumble or complain,
It cannot be acquired by one distraught.
For those who cleared their minds and so forgot
Their worries and distractions (that contain
Concealed impediments), and who abstain
From selfishness will gain what they have sought.
The spirit of the universe will flow
Subconsciously throughout their entire being.
Transcendent relaxation all alone
Will work its magic with a motive, so
That they may feel its purpose, never seeing
That they have gained a power not their own.

There was a great and wise philosopher
Who lived within a regulated mode
And advocated "middle-of-the-road"
Essential rules for all that might occur.
This formal framework served as arbiter
For any problematic episode,
To specify a fair and fitting code
Which might make harmony much likelier.
But this reliance on diplomacy,
Meticulous, precise, exact and rigid,
Was artificial, weak and non-committal
Regarding what transcends humanity.
Propriety and custom seemed too frigid,
A lacquered surface, absolute and brittle.

This wise man symbolized the classical;
He centered on exact, punctilious
Effective rules and ceremony, plus
An emphasis upon the rational.
He always kept in mind the principle
Of compromise, respect and courteous
Humanity toward others, rigorous
Awareness of tradition, ritual.
In contrast to this focus on relations,
The Master looked beyond, at what preceded
Society and human interactions;
He tried imagining divine foundations
Supporting (also factors that impeded)
Our total life, the real and the abstractions.

As if he might examine and disown
The world of real behavior if he stayed,
Contrasting with the kindness he displayed,
The ordinary goodness he had shown,
And which for years had been the cornerstone
Of all he preached (but no one had obeyed),
The Master closed his mind, and unafraid
He left this world, and went away alone.
So mounted on his slow, ungainly beast
He rode across a silent, barren plain
And disappeared without a backward look,
Expecting no reward, but I, at least,
Attempted to envision him again;
But I could not, and so I closed the book.

But ordinary common men existed
Within a world that seemed mysterious;
They sought whatever means they thought assisted
In coping with a global animus.
For consolation and encouragement
Some built upon the ancient superstitions,
Attaching elements now evident
From teachings of the Master, his traditions.
Thus priests arose, relying on belief
In sacred texts to counter doubt and fear,
To channel energy and comfort grief
And cause uncertainty to disappear.
They used this magic power as best they could
To summon higher hosts for human good.

The book itself had never mentioned sin
Nor God, nor prayer, nor need for our salvation;
He preached a way of life, a discipline
That emphasized self-knowledge, meditation.
But ritual and magic, necessary
For reassurance grew, this finally
Begat religion; as a corollary,
The Master then became a deity.
He left me, riding on a buffalo,
And disappeared for all eternity,
But still I lingered on that bleak plateau,
Imagining that in the future he
Beyond my comprehension might ascend
To heaven in the clouds and on the wind.

THE GREAT TEACHER

Just then I sensed a presence close at hand,
A fellow traveler who seemed possessed
With curiosity and interest,
Who stood behind me, and who also scanned
The place the Master disappeared, the land
That rose up to a bare forsaken crest.
He pondered the enigma, then confessed:
"There are some things I do not understand,
The hawk is born to soar across the sky,
The brightly colored fish designed to swim,
The plodding ox to pull a heavy wagon.
I comprehend the creatures who can fly
And those of land or lake, but what of *him*?
He is beyond my knowledge, like a dragon."

We stood a while together in that place
While he was silent, modest, reticent;
His presence seemed to be an accident,
But soon I knew that this was not the case.
Politely he inquired if I would trace
The course that I had followed, different
From his own journey toward enlightenment,
And which had led up to our interface.
I told him of the long and winding route,
The obstacles that I had gone around,
The times I slept, and then would re-awaken,
The many mentors, teachers, all devout,
Their doctrines, both the petty and profound,
The ways I went, and also roads not taken.

He listened patiently as wise men should,
For wisdom mainly lies in comprehension;
And who could judge, not knowing the dimension
Of any problem, or misunderstood
Its implications, whether ill or good?
Should not a teacher pay his strict attention
First to the question, then to intervention,
And give a wise decision if he could?
A tutor with a well-earned reputation
Is one who learned to listen and to wait,
Most certainly to think and analyze
The possible solutions; contemplation
Would clarify his thoughts, alleviate
Confusion, doubt and ill-defined replies.

So only when I finished would he say:
"Throughout my life, I gave much good advice
Of which the sum was true, and all concise,
And none has ever led a man astray.
But many came to me in disarray,
Pursuing magic keys to paradise;
They listened, and reflected on the price
And then, in disappointment, went away.
The ones who came endowed with prejudice
Rejected any wisdom that conflicted
With bigotry that someone else had taught.
The covetous, consumed with avarice,
Would not give up their greed (as I predicted),
Demanding pathways toward the things they sought."

"And then there were the ones who did not care,
Who wandered through their lives so mindlessly
That they could not consent or disagree,
Remaining uninformed and unaware.
Their circumstance, like life itself, unfair,
Implied that like a sea-anemone,
They would be fixed forever, never free
To grow, develop, migrate anywhere.
But there are some (and yes, there have been some),
Who came to me (though some just wandered by),
With open minds, and these sincerely sought
Relief from troubles, and from tedium,
Solutions to the problems that defy
An easy answer, leaving them distraught."

"And you," he said, "are one of those sincere
And honest travelers along the way
That leads from ignorance as night to day,
Who do not ask what they refuse to hear.
Do not expect the answers to be clear
Or free of ambiguity, they may
Confuse the issue, leading you astray;
No one can make these questions disappear.
I cannot change the fact that life is hard,
Nor can you *wish* and have what you prefer.
It matters not how well you might behave,
There is no love that cannot be ill-starred,
No image so exact it has no blur,
No lake so still but that it has its wave."

"In many forms of life, co-operation
Is needed for the species to survive,
As seen with ants, or bees within their hive.
So once with early man, self-preservation
Demanded that complete assimilation
Within the larger circle might deprive
Each single one, but all remained alive;
The group would tolerate no deviation.
Then freedom was inserted like a wedge,
The family of man developed *reason,*
Creating license and autonomy.
Though thinking generated privilege,
Initiative became a form of treason,
And led into a social anarchy."

"When I was young (like you, I once was young),
I found that passion and self-interest
Were motives of us all, the holiest,
The lesser and the average, who wrung
The moral bargains that they lived among
From skirmishes between their unexpressed
But powerful desires; for those obsessed,
They were the only goal to which they clung.
Thus greed and avarice were universal,
And did not represent coincidence,
They were benign if matched by temperance.
But life is real and not a play-rehearsal,
So this behavior had its consequence,
Provoking universal violence.

"With equity in worth assessed so poorly,
Morality and ethics ineffective,
Integrity and honesty elective,
No one could count on anything securely.
For evil comes with life and just as surely,
The world of human souls, the great collective,
Will prove itself incompetent, defective,
Unfit for peace, or to survive maturely.
Because of this, reprisals of the law
(Or threats of this) are always necessary
To govern men, compel them to behave.
When innate virtue fails, then shock and awe
May bring effective (but involuntary)
Direction, as a master and a slave."

"In years gone by, I asked of Han Fei Tzu,
Why rules that rulers make and men accept
Should be so strict, and why they must be kept,
And why each one should care what others do.
'Because the beast of greed turns life into
A cauldron of confusion which (unswept
By discipline), will leave us all inept;
Destructive trends become a witch's brew.
I would reform things for you if I could,
But since I can't, just take them as they are;'
And thus the harsh coercion of the Realists.
But I had hoped that there was something good
Within the soul of man, a glowing star,
And so I sought Mo Tzu and his Idealists."

"This school of thought rejected force and law,
In favor of a love that all-embracing
And universal, ended interlacing
Throughout the lives of men without a flaw.
They said coercion, (like a sheaf of straw
When flung into the wind) would end by chasing
Intended targets randomly, erasing
The benefits the flingers thought they saw.
Instead of looking down as from a shelf
On lesser lives below and judging them
As needing your control, regard each one
Exactly as you feel toward your own self.
Thus none will criticize, or worse, condemn
A person by unfair comparison."

'Regard the plight of others as one's own,
Their persons and their houses and their states.
Become as one who always advocates
An all-inclusive love, the cornerstone
Of all of your endeavor; this alone
Can bring the total peace the world awaits,
And always justifies and validates
The righteous path of life that God has shown.
For there the strong do not oppress the weak,
The honored not disdain the humble, who
Themselves are powerless, as are the poor.
There are no scornful ones to mock the meek,
No brutal mass to overwhelm the few,
Or cunning to deceive the amateur.'

'So universal love, reciprocal
Between all men, regardless of their station
Prevents the tendency to usurpation,
The hallmark of the savage animal.
And likewise with the aboriginal
Of our own species, force's application
Is needed; but when cultured education
Brings total love, this will be pivotal.
Then none will seek to injure one another,
Attacks will cease from greedy feudal lords,
And all will live as one, without complaint.
For who could scorn or dominate his brother,
When harmony creates its own rewards,
And strife and hate are curbed by self-restraint?'

"These are opposed and clashing views, but such
Fit nicely in a narrow pigeon-hole.
Unable by themselves to take control
Of complex human essence, inasmuch
As Law or use of force is like a crutch
Directed toward the sickness, not the soul;
And Love, like Heaven, represents a goal
Toward which a man may strive, but never touch."
These things the Teacher taught; experience
Had shown him that to love is clearly good,
But, isolated, is impractical.
For there will always be a difference
Between the way men act, and how they *should,*
And love is never unconditional.

"There is an ancient axiom: that ice
And embers cannot lie within one bowl;
For one is quenched, the other melts, the whole
Retreats from its polarity, the price
Of balanced unity is sacrifice.
With man, both liberty and self-control
Must forfeit primacy to gain the goal
Of progress toward an earthly paradise.
The use of force is clumsy and degrading,
But love is (by itself) utopian,
And either, unopposed, leads us astray;
The advocates of both are masquerading
As saviors of society, but Man
Would do much better through a Middle Way."

"A compromise is needed to provide
Cohesion for our interactive lives.
The law can license husbands and their wives
In matrimony, and it can decide
Conditions of divorce, which are applied
With cold and solemn logic that deprives
A couple of *affection,*which derives
From love and memory they hold inside.
But all-pervasive love is not enough,
As with an enemy, who does us ill;
Here, justice and a sense of dignity
Are necessary for a rude rebuff.
Reserve benevolence and true good-will
For honest love, without hypocrisy."

"In place of force or love, *benevolence*
Defines the most ideal relationships.
For perfect human-heartedness equips
A man with virtue, moral competence,
Sublime and transcendental, in the sense
That flawless self-possession far outstrips
Component parts, it holds and never slips,
Itself a form of love, without pretense.
This quality produces self-respect,
But equally directed out to others,
It sees the dignity in all creation.
This virtue is exalted, so correct
That speaking of it lightly often smothers
The pure and holy human affirmation".

"Components of benevolence are few,
But all-important: generosity,
Good faith, unselfishness and courtesy,
True diligence in public life, for who
Could separate his moral sense into
One face for all to scan, but secretly
Retain a private insincerity?
Conviction must be constant, through-and-through.
Authentic values mold an attitude
That, obvious to all, communicates
An *empathy*, compassion that survives;
One's own (and private) sentiments include
Regard for everyone that God creates,
And this uniquely can enrich our lives."

"They merit honor, those who can foresee
That circumstances often lie ahead,
Along the road that they and others tread,
Compelling them to share, respectfully.
Achieving this requires maturity,
Unlike the petty, mean, small-spirited
Or selfish person who desires instead
To serve himself without apology.
Humanity, the Person-at-his-Best
Secure within his home, is like a host
Whose visitors are always at their ease,
And likewise in the universe, possessed
Of harmony within his innermost
Existence, will be kind to refugees."

"For self-respect should always generate
Respect for others, not a stratagem
In which one asks: 'what can I get from them?'
But, 'Is there something to alleviate?
How best can I assist, accommodate
And find the crucial source of loss to stem?'
But if too late or futile, not condemn
The foolish, fragile, weak, inadequate.
A host should demonstrate congenial grace,
Composed and certain of his competence,
As stable as a boat with solid keel.
So in this world, one person can erase
Embarrassment with his benevolence,
This is the one who is entirely real."

"If there is righteousness within the heart,
There will be beauty in all characters.
If this is so, then unity occurs
Within each house and home; the counterpart
Of peace and order in the state will start
A process of détente, and travelers
Will carry harmony to foreigners
And elevate agreement to an art.
Thus peace will spread throughout the universe;
There are no boundaries or any borders
To affirmations of one's self and others.
Hostility and discord will disperse,
With tranquil resolution of disorders,
When people are like sisters and like brothers."

"A man achieving true maturity
(Thus making all his actions apropos),
Will never suffer moral vertigo
But focus strictly on propriety.
His words are never incorrect if he
Is careful by his diligence to know
The logic of his case and to forego
Abstract and ill-considered theory.
His manners, simple and appropriate,
Consistent with his speech and attitude
Will demonstrate his grace and savoir-faire.
Sincere behavior, never counterfeit,
Assertive, but not eager to intrude
Is welcome and respected everywhere."

"A reasoned center, constantly between
Unworkable and radical positions
Prevents extravagant extreme conditions,
Which left unmodified or unforeseen
Will bring disaster; these would intervene
To polarize our lives, but inhibitions,
Tending to more moderate traditions
Are based upon the Doctrine of the Mean.
The Constant Middle, therefore, holds dominion
In contrast to unlimited extremes,
Opposing overdoses and excess.
Within this modest sensible opinion
Conceited pride and other foolish dreams
Will fade into the realm of meaningless."

"The Middle Way will check depravity
So early it will not be unrestrained,
Since pride and pleasure both can be contained,
And willfulness become a memory.
Respect for compromise brings harmony
With nothing overdone or unexplained;
Deficiencies can swiftly be regained
And symmetry established easily.
The passion that unbalances our reason
Creates indulgences and overdoses,
Enthusiasm or indifference;
Restraint, like breezes in a summer season
Can clear away the tension and neurosis
Resulting from excess or abstinence."

"Relations must be stable and endure,
Remaining constant, rightly constituted.
No action is conceived or executed
In isolation; through some aperture
Direct and plain, or possibly obscure,
Each move we make, both straight and convoluted
Affects another, and is firmly rooted
In parallel with bonds that are secure.
These binding links must be so well-defined
That each relationship is confident
Of where within the web one's place will be,
And what response one may expect to find
With any statement or a mild dissent,
And so preserve good form and honesty."

"Both parents have a duty to their child
To love and nurture him while he is young;
But even more, the source to which he'd clung
Is due respect, devotion reconciled
To all the history they have compiled.
And thus the fountain from which virtue sprung
Contains the key for all who live among
Confused events, all seemingly defiled.
For only family can elevate
The animal (or primitive) existence
Into a higher level which could take
The web of life and truly animate
The spirit of a great benevolence,
To clarify a mirror once opaque."

"The senior member of a pair is gentle,
So he himself in turn will be respected;
A faithful wife should never be neglected
But in return be more than ornamental.
Successful unions are not accidental,
Whenever imperfections are detected,
No criticism should be misdirected
Or patronizing, seemingly parental.
With family and friends much care is needed
To keep relations cordial, understood;
An older sibling must be firm but kind,
His good advice should never go unheeded.
The younger, deferential, always should
Make certain that the two are well-aligned."

"An older friend is helpful as a mentor
If younger ones will truly pay attention
And try to minimize their apprehension,
Abstaining from the role of rude dissenter.
Experienced, enlightened men who enter
Into a teacher's role, a new dimension,
Must side-step any hint of condescension
And keep discreet control within their center.
The ruler of a state who is despotic
Will lose his ethical imperative,
And cannot then demand obedience;
But if he is benign and patriotic
The citizens must be affirmative
With lasting loyalty and confidence."

"When such relationships are firm and true
And in their proper balance, they will be
An indicator, and a vital key
To social order, serving as the glue.
Whenever chaos came and overthrew
A house and ruptured its stability,
Examination showed conclusively
Its symmetry already was askew.
For when adhesive slips or fails to hold,
And complicated parts are re-arranged,
The total structure loses permanence;
Connections to the center, uncontrolled,
No longer sound, but broken or deranged,
Will seek new pathways, causing turbulence."

"So, central to stability, tradition
Prescribes reliance on what has before
Been shown to be effective, to restore
Integrity and valid intuition.
So each new undertaking or ambition
Must meet the test of time and not ignore
The records of the past that underscore
The value of recall and repetition.
For through the ages, all that man has done
Can be attributed to his own will,
But must be modified by great respect
For patterns of behavior that, begun
In generations past, have proven still
To be productive, prudent and correct."

"The young should have a deep regard for age
As worthy of respect and veneration;
Advancing years have one great compensation,
For wisdom is a crucial heritage
Transmitted through unbroken lineage.
Experience has been the firm foundation
Of sound decisions; pure imagination
And youth may use this gift for leverage.
Maturity has gained intrinsic worth
By earning a perspective through the years,
But also forfeiting impulsiveness.
Unlimited potential seen at birth
Has narrowed but has deepened and appears
As judgment which the young do not possess."

"Each quandary has its unique conclusion,
Through every maze there is one certain way;
Tradition in itself may often sway
Behavior that seems destined for confusion.
But blind reliance on the past, profusion
Of lessons memorized just yesterday
But which unseen developments betray,
Will lead to error, and at worst, delusion.
Intelligence must modify convention,
Interpreting the lessons of the past;
So that in times of discord, chaos, strife,
The proper attitude and comprehension
Will indicate directions unsurpassed
As models for the well-conducted life."

"Propriety, the sense of what is right,
Is learned through difficult experience;
Alert involvement, done with diligence
Ensures awareness for the neophyte.
But some, those guilty of an oversight,
Or burdened with a mental indolence,
Will pay a price for this indifference
By living on within a moral blight.
If this seems harsh, stupidity is worse;
A dunce is always destined to repeat
The lessons in his life he has not learned.
This constant failure can become a curse,
And each experience a dead-end street,
With neither benefit nor wisdom earned."

"Intelligence, however, finds a road
That followed faithfully brings resonance,
Avoiding hardships caused by ignorance
But not requiring any episode
That in and of itself might overload
The opportunity for relevance
With painful incident or circumstance
That would a proper attitude corrode.
This pathway is the one of right decision
Before the very first initial test,
So one may be rehearsed in his perspective,
Prepared to act with powerful precision.
This situation is the very best
And also is the one that is effective."

"Successful life depends upon tradition,
The patterns of behavior that have shown
A promising and upright cornerstone
On which to build a flourishing position.
The lessons of the past, by definition,
Can shape our attitudes to form a clone
Of past experience, as if on loan
To future generations in transition.
Not all of history is fortunate,
Some actions are superb and some in error.
Precursors, wise or favored, may be rich
While others, luckless or inadequate
May end in poverty, with guilt or terror;
The secret is deciding which is which."

"Incompetent or even evil deeds
May seem at first to lead to good effects;
But later, on inspection one detects
A central flaw which everyone concedes.
To follow such a pattern only leads
To foolish mimicry which misdirects
The honest effort that each man expects
In searching for sincere authentic creeds.
But lives that first appear unpromising
May prove on second, close analysis
To demonstrate the key to righteous living;
So if experience means anything
It must be clearly seen as genesis
Of qualities both lasting and life-giving."

"Recorders of the past are necessary
But equally they must be analyzed,
To separate the sound from ill-advised,
Well-founded from the mere imaginary.
Antiquity can be contemporary
For history, seen clearly, undisguised,
Can serve as proper guidance, summarized
Into a code, a moral sanctuary.
Adopting critical intelligence
To keep the forces of tradition whole,
A teacher can interpret, modify,
Combine the past with current common sense,
And by this alteration can control
The attitudes on which we all rely."

"Propriety, or what is right, a plan
For regulated conduct through the course
Of long and complicated lives will force
Alignment with a formula that can
Provide the guidance over any span
Of circumstance, of failure or divorce;
And in a time of victory a source,
A sense of what should guide a gentleman.
Our lives are stylized, a sacred dance,
With music and with choreography,
The patterns are predictable, foreseen;
If these are formulated in advance
A principle develops, which will be
Our guide to living, tranquil and serene."

"A ruler must be like a gentle wind,
For people are as fields of grass or grain;
A breeze that blows across a quiet plain
Will alter which direction they will bend.
To govern, therefore, is to comprehend
That virtue, both consistent and humane,
Is like the polar star, which will remain
In its own place, and on which all depend.
A leader may be powerful and strong
And rule by force alone, but not at length;
Inherent righteousness should animate
His soul, for it must be there all along.
The greatest power then is moral strength
In people who are orderly and straight."

"The arts of peace will elevate the mind
And culture will exalt the human soul;
Serenity increases self-control
With intellect and virtue intertwined.
Barbarity is often re-aligned
Into civility (a greater goal
Than conquest for a people as a whole),
By education and the arts combined.
While music soothes the spirit's agitation
Replacing foolish anger with tranquility,
By poetry the mind can be aroused,
Inducing insight by imagination,
And teach the higher art of sensibility,
Perfect the dwelling where our soul is housed."

"The test of cultures, of society
Is moral character, the excellence
Of serving one another, evidence
Of conscience, ethics and philosophy.
The proof of people is their energy
In self-improvement, and their diligence
In striving for the great experience
Of fully sensing human harmony.
There is no *self* apart from social links,
Each human being lives within a web,
Relations are the center of our lives.
The moral person studies and re-thinks
The constant flow, the surging and the ebb,
Cross-currents where humanity survives."

"Becoming fully human means transcending
A long and winding sequence of mistakes,
The arrogance which constantly forsakes
Our egos when we know we are pretending.
It means rejecting all that is offending,
In favor of the silence that awakes
Illumination of the soul, and makes
A synthesis beyond our comprehending.
Thus, Man is not the measure of all things;
But humanism (all embracing strength)
Becomes much deeper and more satisfying,
Immune to failures and to weakenings
When bound to sacred images, at length
Providing endless peace beyond denying."

"Somewhere within our present universe
A power on the side of righteousness
Exists, and gives to every man access
To Heaven, into which he may immerse.
For man must unify and not disperse
His human spirit, and must coalesce
Into the 'Will of Heaven' to express
The finer parts of life, and not the worse.
The Trinity of *Heaven, Man and Earth*
Is not discovered with divining rods,
Nor does it constitute a passageway
To total bliss, but still it has its worth.
If you deny or so displease the gods,
To whom in times of trouble will you pray?"

"But all we know in life is what we know,
And we are ignorant of all the rest;
We speculate on spirits, at our best
Creating some divine scenario.
But at our worst, we often think we owe
A sacrifice or service to attest
That in return we hope we may be blessed,
And all the while ignore the status quo.
How can one serve the spirits of the dead
Before assisting those who, all around,
Require our help for sickness and for grief,
The needs that all of us inherited?
First we must live the life that we have found,
And care for troubles that require relief."

He built a structure based upon tradition,
And on examples of a moral power;
But these are brittle, and the world's ambition
Stood ready to disrupt and to deflower.
For memory is tenuous at best,
And rituals are fragile, all depending
Upon believers, who have acquiesced
To solemn rites, not fully comprehending.
He saw the changes no one could avoid
And listened as the prophecy was spoken:
In time the edifice would be destroyed,
Supporting beams would finally be broken;
While far away, the Sacred Mountain fell,
The wisest of all teachers said farewell.

THE ENLIGHTENED ONE

Then as I went again along my way,
I saw a man who sat beneath a tree
And seemed the essence of serenity.
He smiled with confidence, as if to say
If I had wandered, lost and far-astray
That I was welcome in his company;
And if my spirit felt imprisoned, he
Would offer access to a passageway.
I did not understand his calm restraint,
Nor his authority through his quiescence,
And so I sought to lessen my mistake.
"If not a god, an angel or a saint,
Then what are you?" I asked, "What is your essence?"
He merely said to me, "I am awake."

"The world is wrapped within a womb of sleep
Where waking consciousness is but a dream,
And all endeavor toward a self-esteem
Will merely demonstrate how very deep
Awareness can be shrouded, and how steep
The climb to sensitivity may seem,
How difficult the pathway to redeem
Our moral lives as anything but sheep.
Too many lead a closed, constricted life
Without an exit, destitute of light,
A cold and wintry place of discontent,
Where ritual solutions are as rife
As they are ineffective; to recite
A liturgy is not enlightenment."

I recognized his gracious invitation
And sat with him, expecting to be taught
Solutions and the answers I had sought,
At least receive some useful information.
But he was silent, deep in contemplation,
Immersed within his own internal thought;
Observing him at length, I felt I ought
To spend an equal time in preparation.
With stillness hanging thickly in between,
The two of us then sat in peace together;
Potential still was there, inviolate
As were his promises, but unforeseen,
One problem still continued, as to whether
An uncommitted mind could concentrate.

I cannot say how long we meditated
(At least he did), I only tried to keep
My intellect from wandering, to sweep
The frivolous aside, suppress unstated
Impulses, stimuli that violated
The blankness I attempted, but which creep
Into the mind, as dreams will do in sleep;
Thus, mental vacuums are complicated.
But finally, instead of random flashes
My memories aligned in parallel,
Receding far ahead in true perspective
Without the accidental aimless clashes
And cross-connections that ideas compel
To render concentration ineffective.

Then slowly I began to realize
The benefit a contemplative mind
Could bring to anyone who was inclined
To cleanse the soul of foolish and unwise
Self-centered inclinations that arise
Incessantly when life is undefined;
The silence and the openness combined
Correct the faults we might not recognize.
These flaws include desire and lust and craving,
Delusion and hostility and pride,
Obsessive patterns that destroy our peace,
That cause depression, overt misbehaving,
And secret inner fancies that misguide
Our outer lives into a mere caprice.

But I could not say clearly how I knew
The things I learned while sitting there with him;
He spoke in threads of thought, the interim
Was silence, thus the total picture grew
By meditation on the residue
Of meanings he suggested, sometimes dim
Initially, when forming on the rim
Of central brilliance, later seen as true.
I learned to listen to an aphorism
And then to let it permeate my mind,
Allowing it to crystallize until
I could recite, as in a catechism
A simple concept which would be refined
As purely as reflection could distill.

At last my mind was ready to receive
Instruction, I would follow where it led
(I hoped that I could fathom what he said),
For this was my ambition: to retrieve
The essence of his teaching, and achieve
The high serenity I coveted;
And so he spun for me his "noble thread"
Which I, within, was ready to believe.
But this at once proved more than troublesome,
My efforts ending in futility,
My past and present life an obstacle;
For only in a final state to come,
The human spirit's highest destiny,
Nirvana, would this peace be possible.

To God or gods he was indifferent,
Accepting Deity as an ideal
(Not totally denying it is real),
But only saying it is impotent;
If it exists, it is an accident
That has no strength to intervene or heal,
Unknowable, unable to reveal
Itself as kindly or benevolent.
Denying all the supernatural,
He would, if asked, dismiss as visionary
A mystic firmament-in-parallel,
Rejecting firmly as nonsensical
The Universe of Dante Alighieri
Containing Heaven, Purgatory, Hell.

Into a world without divine control,
(Theology without a deity),
A place of constant flux and vagrancy,
He placed psychology without a soul.
For in this earthly life he found no role
For permanence or certain destiny,
But only whirl and change and urgency
Without a metaphysics or a goal.
Our lives repeat themselves in random ways,
But all are dominated by affliction;
Our birth itself is painful and traumatic,
Each age of life thereafter is a phase
Of added dislocation and constriction
Until despair and sorrow are emphatic.

"Of Noble Truths, therefore, this is the first:
That all our lives are filled with suffering,
From early years decline is threatening,
Vitality is constantly reversed.
Each loss reminds us that our lives are cursed
With hopes that endlessly are vanishing,
Security and love unraveling;
Of all of these, the dread of death is worst.
But meanwhile, to be fixed to what you fear,
Or find that one you loved has gone away,
Is equally distressing to the soul;
And sickness (which may suddenly appear),
Rejection, pain and failure all convey
The threat of dissolution of the whole."

"These factors all are sad, unfortunate,
But true and manifest, they do exist,
Yet should not generate a pessimist.
For all is well if as a counterweight
We understand the pain of life as fate,
But one which we can consciously resist
By understanding, thus the analyst
Can find the cause before it is too late.
What is the cause of insecurity,
The reason life is often unfulfilling?
The rift, the source of our estranged condition
Is thinking of our private destiny.
Protecting ego-strength, we are unwilling
To sacrifice our personal ambition."

"If we are unenlightened and succumb
To selfish or to personal desire,
And focus on the things we can acquire
We lose our basic equilibrium.
As if surviving in a vacuum
We float directionless, and our entire
Relations with reality expire,
Becoming non-specific tedium.
So we must realize that Life is One,
That selfishness will contradict this Law;
Our egos will, of course, provide resistance,
Pursuing incandescence like the sun.
The second Truth: to recognize this flaw
That ruptures harmony in our existence."

"When facing this dilemma, wise men would
Endeavor to reduce or off-set pain,
The dislocation that our lives contain,
Preventing disappointment if they could.
To create comfort from distress they should
Identify the ways we live in vain,
The sources of our sorrow, then abstain
From everything that does not lead to good.
Because we know that private enterprise
(Without regard to universal kindness)
Will lead to selfish craving and despair,
The cure that noble wisdom would advise
Is overcoming egotistic blindness
And see all life as equal, everywhere."

"If we appreciate this axiom,
We will have found a Noble Truth, the third,
To guide our course, and thus will have deterred
Ourselves from lives both bleak and troublesome.
Indulgence makes the human spirit numb
But abstinence may also be absurd,
Asceticism is a dismal word,
Its ultimate will cause delirium.
So we must find a compromise between
Extremes of comfort and of self-denial,
Renouncing foolish narcissistic pleasure
While rationing the needs that can be seen.
The Middle Way deserves an honest trial
If either pole has proved a faulty measure."

"And now the problem has been recognized,
Along with its importance in our lives;
We know our equanimity survives
By grace of difficulties analyzed.
We may detect conditions once disguised
And hidden when our selfishness deprives
The liberated life (which only thrives
By self-control) of what is greatly prized.
The fourth of Noble Truths brings evolution
Of ways we can escape captivity
From narrow limits to a vast expanse
Of tranquil life, obtaining absolution
By virtue of abstaining faithfully
From craving, vanity and arrogance."

"We find on every journey that we make
(Including life itself) that we must choose
Before beginning, pathways we will use
To reach our goal; and if we fail to take
A proper guide (or foolishly forsake
Considered wisdom), often we will lose
The landmarks, guideposts and the overviews
That keep our way apparent, not opaque.
To travel in an unreflective way
By random impulse and by circumstance
Is like a leaf gyrating in the wind.
But well-intentioned living will display
(If practiced faithfully) a resonance,
A harmony, a course we comprehend."

"Preparing for the passage leading out
From narrow limits of self-interest
Where life is anxious, narrow and distressed
Into a place of certainty throughout,
Each one must choose a mentor, wise, devout
Who has already followed in his quest
The principles that proved to serve him best,
And who will reassure and lessen doubt.
Just as a bee cannot exist alone
(Its social unit always is the hive),
We humans make no progress on the Way
Without supportive networks of our own.
We need their calm assurance to survive,
The guidance and compassion they convey."

"If you have found the province of concern,
Consideration, love and confidence
(That is provided with benevolence
By such a guide), you must attempt to learn
The path that leads to truth, and to discern
The eight components which experience
Has shown as central, and will influence
Achievement of the goal we all must earn.
Associate with mentors such as these
And listen to their wisdom as they say
Essential things that you must know to fashion
A higher life that liberates and frees
The spirit from constraint; observe the way
They live their lives with love and with compassion."

"And thus prepared, you may begin," he said,
"Your journey from the darkness into light;
But keep your counselor within your sight,
And do not run too fast or far ahead.
For in pursuit of what you coveted,
A superficial charismatic might
Put forward to a naïve acolyte
Some flight of fancy that he heralded.
So keep your holy mentor close at hand,
Associate with him, observe his ways,
Converse with him, absorb his mode of living,
Adjust your own toward it, and understand
The difficulty of the endless maze
Of faithless life, forever unforgiving."

"The journey of a thousand miles or more
Begins with simple steps; the right direction
Is critical, and so complete reflection
Is always indicated long before
Beginning odysseys (that heretofore,
Arising after meager introspection
Would often meet with failure and rejection),
Thus, planning is the concept to restore.
The Noble Truths will show you where you are,
The errors in your present regimen,
And how to temper these when you decide
To travel through a strange and singular
Experience, succeeding only when
The Eightfold Path is followed as a guide."

"The step that follows this analysis
Is to decide if we have true intent,
And whether what we said is what we meant;
Distraction by our human avarice,
May undermine our fragile edifice.
Our resolution must be confident
Not merely what is now convenient,
Nor subject to a whim or prejudice.
As kites in gusty winds will swirl and dip
Without an anchor, cartwheel to the ground,
And cancel all the beauty of their flight,
Temptation causes our resolve to slip
Unless our dedication is profound,
And concentration resolutely bright."

"We must take care of language and our speech,
For what we say reveals our character,
As in the instances when we may blur
The goals we seek, so these stay out of reach.
Deceit and guile are foolish, they will teach
Our inner selves to be a prisoner
In fear of openness, and will recur
Until we see the damage done by each.
The walls our egos build will thus constrict
Our sense of who we are, until they touch
Our very center, then we realize
How deep is our descent, how derelict
Integrity becomes; we lose as much
As we have tried to gain, and all we prize."

"Not only honesty, but kindness too
Must be the essence of our whole expression,
For neither slander nor an 'indiscretion'
Nor gossip (whether valid or untrue)
Allows our own development into
A gracious, steady gradual progression
Toward ideal states of perfect self-possession
Where charity and courtesy ensue.
If, reaching further back to *motivation*
(The central source of conscious and impulsive
Remarks and actions scattered thickly through
Our lives as seen by others), exploration
Reveals intentions, worthy or repulsive
That govern things we do, or do not do."

"Before a person changes how they act
They need to understand their inner soul,
And how subconscious thinking can control
Their speech and actions, even if abstract.
Within endeavors that we all enact
How much is due to kindness, on the whole?
How much to hope of praise, which some extol?
(These are the ones dissembling will attract).
But for some rules there are no substitutes,
Nor can a person plead his ignorance,
A few behaviors cannot be erased.
These principles remain as absolutes:
Do not indulge in strong intoxicants,
Nor kill or steal or lie or be unchaste."

"A story of an early Russian Czar
Maintains that he was choosing for his state
A single faith that would accommodate
Himself and also prove so popular
That this religion in particular
Would by itself be fully adequate
And never need another alternate;
He had a single benchmark, quite bizarre.
He studied Islam, its entirety
Compared to Christ and Buddha, for a sign;
And when he found it, suddenly forgot
Their doctrines, ethics and theology.
He chose the Christians, Jesus liked his wine,
While Buddha and the Prophet, they did not."

"What calling best promotes our total lives,
And which career allows one's self to grow?
A true profession is a sign we know
What nourishes our spirit, what deprives
Our character of goals toward which it strives.
For total liberation, one must go
Into monastic orders, even though
In other occupations virtue thrives.
These must contain a moral excellence,
A core of honor into which one delves
In search of harmony, avoiding strife;
For even when pursued with diligence
Careers are never ends unto themselves
But are an entry to a better life."

"Achieving any goal involves exertion,
Maintaining it requires an endless will.
You may secure objectives once, but still
Upholding them demands prolonged assertion.
At every step you must avoid diversion,
Have strength and patience if the road uphill
Is longer, steeper than you knew, until
You reach the distant end of your excursion.
Along the way you will have passed the ones
Impatient with a slow and steady pace
Who ran too far too fast, and stopped to rest
And never then continued, simpletons
Who treated life as if it were a race
Instead of as a never-ending quest."

"All things are mastered by our mindfulness,
And all we are results from all we've thought;
If we could *understand* the things we ought,
Then life itself would cause us no distress.
When ignorance is all that we possess
We find ourselves disturbed and over-wrought;
The remedy is our awareness, taught
By self-examination, limitless.
So be aware of every action taken,
Discard obsessive, harmful prototypes,
Release the cruel longings and self-pity
That leave a gentle character forsaken.
For there are many moral guttersnipes
Whose principles at best are far from pretty."

"You reach awareness through regeneration,
A time allowing nothing to distract,
Not grievances or fears that can impact
The purity of total concentration.
Nor should your longings or anticipation,
Or hopes or dreams, or any other fact
Intrude upon your mind, nor any act
That interferes with deeper meditation.
As seeds inert within the ground will rot,
You must be liberated, and arise
In order that you may be saved from blindness.
You can not see at all if you cannot
See beauty, which will help to harmonize
Your heart and mind with perfect loving kindness."

"How then should we interpret transmigration?
And what about the human self is real,
What part of it is finite, what ideal,
Is there a thread of infinite causation?
The human spirit is a combination:
Inheritance, a culture's balance-wheel,
Links generations but cannot conceal
A free and conscious *will* in motivation;
This is an essence *used* but not used up.
It travels through a space and stays the same,
It changes, yet it bears an unchanged stamp,
As holy water poured from cup to cup,
Anoints a king, or as a single flame
Is transferred from a candle to a lamp."

"The culmination, if we were to trace
This process of renewal to the end,
Would be the point in time when thoughts transcend
Their limits and expand the commonplace
Into a heightened, all-inclusive space.
Here, all is clear and honest, none pretend,
A state the ignorant misapprehend
And some have even called a burnt-out case.
This state is called Nirvana, and consists
Of absence of our energy and pain
And though like wind it scorns analysis,
Legitimate, authentic, it exists.
The flame extinguished, this will still remain,
The essence that survives, eternal bliss."

"Your life is not with permanence endowed,
A star at dawn, a ripple in a stream,
A flash of lightning in a summer cloud,
A flickering lamp, a phantom and a dream.
As waves are re-created and recur
(While one disperses others will begin),
The years will pass and you, a traveler
Will search in vain for refuge at an inn.
But when you make your crossing, all is changed;
The flow of time is now irrelevant,
Your view of all your life is rearranged,
And grief and heartache insignificant.
Your freedom from the finite will at last
Be endless future from an endless past."

"Be grateful for your journey, and the river
That separates the ancient from the new;
Respect the guides and boats which will deliver
You safely from the world which you outgrew.
The land that you are leaving, one of change
And ignorance and selfishness and pain
Is nonetheless familiar, while the strange
And distant shore is mystical terrain.
That place has wisdom and enlightenment,
Although at first obscure and ill-defined;
It will become more focused, evident
As you approach, your outlook re-aligned.
So board the ferry, let the present go
Awareness now is all you need to know."

Then he again was silent, in his hand
He held a single flower overhead,
A golden lotus, which was meant instead
Of words to show what I must understand.
I watched and felt my consciousness expand
As if the world which I inhabited
Was now too small, and (though it was unsaid),
Should be continued in another land.
I gazed upon the lotus, and I knew
Serenity, for beauty rested there,
Yet not the kind that anyone possessed;
For all could have a corresponding view,
And all who contemplated were aware
That something changed that could not be expressed.

My mind, once poorly focused, now was clear;
Adjustments had been made and I could see
Delusion, craving and hostility
As evils of the past, they disappear
As nightmares into morning atmosphere.
The perfect way knows only harmony
With no euphoria, no misery,
And nothing in excess or too austere.
But if we linger here, then we are lost,
Wherever on the shore that we may roam
We find the errors that we must erase.
So ultimately, rivers must be crossed,
Another country is our future home,
Enlightenment is in a different place.

And so it was, the past began to fade,
Its images, now blurred, released their hold,
And many factors, which had once conveyed
Significance to life (as was foretold),
Became irrelevant, now out of sight,
But still the farther shore did not appear.
And in this interval, my only light
Was refuge in the one who had been here,
Who was my guide, and in the sturdy boat
On which my life depended, and the crew,
Their order and their skill to keep afloat
In transit from the old into the new.
But even when I reached the other side
And understood, I was not satisfied.

The pathway he had shown seemed incomplete,
Although in part it served the seeker well;
Awakening had proven bittersweet,
Contentment and frustration parallel.
Tranquility required renunciation
Of striving and endeavors I had known,
Replacing active life with contemplation,
Discarding all ambitions of my own.
In this, I sensed that I had found the flaw
In honest, principled austerity;
I would engage the world and not withdraw,
And so I left him there beneath his tree.
Enlightened though he was, he still forgot:
Serenity is passive, life is not.

THE PATRIARCH

Then from a forest, dense, forbidding, dark,
A voice: "Repent", it cried, "Make straight the way".
Exactly who it was I could not say,
But sensed a prophet, priest or patriarch.
And then the man himself, with every mark
Of education, eloquence that lay
Beneath his moral passion to convey
A judgment and a message; both were stark.
"All you, like sheep, have gone astray and turned
To your own path, ignoring or rejecting
The Lord's command for pure morality,
His holy offering which you have spurned."
I looked around behind me, half-expecting
A sinful crowd, but there was only me.

Apparently, he sensed that he was rude,
And coming closer, he apologized,
"My greeting certainly was ill-advised,
But often I confront ingratitude.
The People of the Lord have misconstrued
His Holy Will, at times have scandalized
Propriety, and God has agonized
About their conduct, insolent and crude.
So I (and many others) have been sent
To search for sinful people, to remind
Them that their God again is intervening.
My mission is to cry: 'Awake, repent,'
So they may turn again and all may find
That Holiness and righteous life have meaning."

"The earth and sky must hear what I am saying:
The Lord of all, who never has withheld
His generosity, unparalleled,
Has looked upon His people disobeying
The very covenant that was displaying
His favor and His love, which far excelled
In worthiness these people, who rebelled,
Defying righteousness and seldom praying.
Their holy days, their rites and sacrifices
Are emptiness until their hands are clean;
Their lives that shone so brightly now are dull
Their chronicles a catalog of vices.
I have been sent once more to intervene,
But remedies require a miracle."

"First they must come and listen to the Lord,
Who says to them to wash their hands, their lives,
So when the day of reckoning arrives
They will receive His favor and reward.
To earn this state of heavenly accord
Each one must wake, and live as one who strives
For justice, so that equity survives;
They must avoid the sin that God abhorred.
And moving past this abstract rectitude
The righteous must take care of those oppressed,
The orphans and the widows who, alone,
Would have no chance, but always be pursued
By charlatans who cleverly assessed
Their isolation, taking all they own."

"The people, once like silver, now are dross,
They are but water where there once was wine;
The filigree of life, the Lord's design
Is knotty now, chaotic, without gloss.
But even in the face of such a loss
There still is hope; if they will re-align
Their wicked lives with that which is divine,
There always is a bridge they may re-cross.
If so, appearances will then be glistening,
The water may become good wine again,
The stains of scarlet made as white as wool.
The people of the Lord must first be listening,
And then must pay attention, say 'Amen'
And recognize their Lord is merciful."

"In days to come the highest place of all
Will be the mountain where the Temple stands,
And towering above the hills commands
The nations of the world, both great and small.
And all shall come, the false and cynical,
The fierce, the warlike of the many lands
In order that their righteousness expands
Until they all are ecumenical.
The Lord will teach them all the arts of peace,
And settle the disputes between great nations,
To create concord as the Law allows,
And wars and hostile competitions cease.
The Lord's own genuine adjudications
Will make them hammer swords and shields to plows."

"Then nations never more will go to war,
Creating battles over all the earth;
The tribes of man will have a second birth,
Now free of greed and arrogance that mar
The love of God, and in particular
Condemn us all to scarcity and dearth.
For trust in mortal man, what is it worth?
Observance of the Law shines like a star.
The Lord Himself compels humility,
Deflating all the proud and the conceited.
Their fortresses, with all their walls and towers
Dismantled, lose defensibility;
Their idols are demolished and defeated,
For thus the Lord will demonstrate His powers."

"Come, listen to a story I will tell:
I saw the Lord, exalted and most high
And He has sent me here to certify
His grandeur and His love, in parallel.
His strength is like a mighty citadel
Which can resist attack from earth or sky;
But delicately as a dragonfly,
He hovers near us like a sentinel.
He makes the plants and trees throughout the land
Grow large and beautiful, producing fruit
Sustaining all the cities, every county.
Whatever any person might demand
Or wish, unsaid, the Lord is resolute,
And will provide our needs out of His bounty."

"This land of milk and honey, though, depends
Upon the people's willingness to choose
A righteous path, and never to misuse
The gift of life and all its dividends.
For God, in all His graciousness, intends
That men appreciate and not abuse
What they receive; the Lord will not excuse
An inner arrogance, that condescends.
The pride of man is like Jerusalem,
Which in its time the center of the world,
Became a law unto itself, ignoring
The Lord, who could bestow or could condemn,
Depending on behavior, and who hurled
His wrath upon the ones beyond restoring."

"There was a vineyard on a sunny hill,
And when the fields were cleared of every stone,
The earth was plowed, the owner all alone
Selected all the vines that then would fill
His fertile land. He chose them with great skill,
The finest only, those which had been shown
To yield a fruitful harvest when full-grown;
He worked his vineyard with the best of will.
He built a hedge and towers to surround
The valued land, with walls of many shapes
To keep the animals (which would devour
The tender grapes) away, then in the ground
He dug a pit in which to tread the grapes;
Then came the harvest, every grape was sour."

"He asked his friends: 'The fault, is it in me?
Perhaps instead, the vineyard is to blame,
For somehow, grapes that should be fine became
Undrinkable and sour, how can this be?
I cared for them with great ability,
The ground was good, the vines were prime, the same
As those producing vintages that claim
Without exception, splendid quality.
And yet I gathered in a lesser growth
Than I had every reason to expect,
An entire harvest has been ruined, lost.'
And so the vintner devastated both
The field and all the vines; the architect
Undid what he created at such cost."

"The farmer thus uprooted all the vines
And took away the towers and the hedge
That shielded all his land around the edge,
Removing this deserted vineyard's signs.
He gave the feral deer and porcupines,
The rabbits and the goats the privilege
To trample what was left and then to dredge
The roots of plants that would not make good wines.
When he had cleared the remnants from the field
The weeds invaded, brambles and a brier
To cover barren ground with thorns and clover.
In order to obtain a better yield,
A quality he hoped would be much higher,
He had resolved to start completely over."

"The Lord, however, is more generous.
He sees the people stumbling in the dark,
A land of shadows, barren, bleak and stark,
Where many are both drunk and gluttonous.
The lives they lead are foolish, frivolous,
Without a light or one redeeming spark,
Descending in a long and endless arc
Toward closure, sinful and idolatrous.
Aware of this, the Lord will still forgive
The ones who cease to linger in the night,
But turn again and seek a better way.
He will allow the penitent to live,
And shine upon the wanderers a light
Illuminating all they might survey."

"The *Will of God* is therefore good, kind-hearted,
His energy and power will converge
With love and with compassion and emerge
A unity that never has been charted.
Before all human history had started,
The Mind of God conceived the vital urge;
Creation then proceeded with a surge
So powerful that it could not be thwarted.
Nor has it yet been modified by men;
Through all of life, its concept and its sequel,
No prince on earth, not emperors nor czars
Have moved God's will one inch, so even when
Our dreams and lives diverge and are unequal
The fault is in ourselves, and not the stars."

"The world is good because God made it good,
And therefore living has intrinsic worth.
The greatest evil anywhere on earth,
Indifference, not doing what one should,
Denies divine intentions, and it could
Lead on to nonsense, folly and to mirth,
To even darker elements, the birth
Of blasphemy and sin in likelihood.
Despite this risk, the righteousness of God
Is constant, faithful, true and everlasting,
Both slow to anger, eager to forgive;
And as a wonderful divining rod
Seeks water, He seeks virtue, thus contrasting
His love and holiness with how we live."

"Then what is man? He is a blend of dust
And of divinity, both weak and frail;
He by himself must always fade and fail,
Consumed by greed and selfishness and lust.
He can regain his self-respect by trust
In God who will forgive, and will unveil
A glory and an honor on a scale
Undreamed of, and an essence pure and just.
Conversion from a life of fear and weakness
To one of grandeur, sanctity and brightness
May seem a hope that common reason bars;
And yet the Lord Himself conceived uniqueness
For all mankind, a state of perfect lightness
And just a little lower than the stars."

"The Lord, through Moses and the prophets spoke:
'Avoiding evil, find the path to good.
I call to earth, to heaven, that they should
Be witness to the covenants you broke
And I restored; believers who awoke
To contemplate their futures understood
That even if they did the best they could,
They still depended on a master-stroke.
I live within you, outside, overhead,
And I, who at the outset gave you breath
Divide your options now, as with a knife,
Into your last alternative,' he said;
'Thus I have set before you life and death,
And I will say to you and yours, choose life'."

"How *should* you live, then, given His command
And His example of benevolence,
But with a strict observance, reverence,
Avoiding all the acts that He has banned?
The Law is still the core of what He planned,
And this allows no disobedience,
No variation and no arguments;
The prophets came to help you understand.
For you must be a light to all the world,
To clear the eyes of all who have been blind;
To liberate from dungeons, from the dark,
The prisoners of ignorance who hurled
Themselves into the place they are confined,
Rejecting counsels of their patriarch."

"Within the Scriptures, Laws, and Testaments
There are six hundred thirteen admonitions,
Some merely cautions, others prohibitions
Of serious or difficult events.
They regulate behavior, incidents
That would displease the Lord, besides conditions
Exalting earthly piety, positions
Of unity with God, and penitence.
These rules, when vague or somewhat esoteric
Require a priest or rabbi to explain
God's perfect and transparent regimen.
But some compelling mandates are generic
And to the whole of human life pertain;
Of these, the Great Commandments, there are ten."

"The Great Commandment (whence all others flow),
Is: 'Love the Lord with all your heart and mind,
And have no other deities'; mankind,
Obeying Him and loving Him will know
The mercy of the Lord, from long ago
To generations yet to come, and find
Eternal peace, security designed
To make it seem like Heaven here below.
An idol would offend His holy sight,
The Lord thy God cannot be represented
And therefore graven images are false.
His essence is of power, love and light,
A single *will*, supreme, unprecedented,
Which life and all the universe exalts."

"The name of God is holy and unique,
And never is to be referred to lightly,
Nor used in phrases that could impolitely
Display a mean, antagonistic streak.
Nor should appeals to God be used to sneak
A personal assistance, even slightly;
To skew the Will of God into unsightly
Advantage is unethical and weak.
The purpose of the Lord is not to grant
A favor to the one who calls His name,
Support a faction or to interface
In petty quarrels, please the supplicant.
Nor can the ones who publicly proclaim
Devotion to the Lord expect His grace."

"He does not need your Temple sacrifices,
And when you lift your hands in public prayer
He will not look at you, or be aware
Until your hands and heart are clean; your vices
Speak louder than your offerings, devices
Like incense, holy days and vows you swear
(Hypocrisy that He can hardly bear)
Are false, while simple purity suffices.
To pay attention to what God is teaching
Is critical as far as righteousness.
Stop doing evil, learn how to be good,
Renounce those priests whose superficial preaching
May promise favored treatment or access
To God Himself, and do those things you should."

"Observe the Sabbath, always keep it holy.
He will allow six days for your vocation,
To do your work and tend your occupation
No matter how exalted or how lowly.
The seventh, though, belongs to Him, and wholly,
In honor of the end of God's Creation;
And therefore all within your habitation
Must rest and worship Him, and do this solely.
Within this life that you are given, strive
To honor both your father and your mother,
That you may live to old and honored age,
Respected for your wisdom, and may thrive."
And here I heard the echoes of another,
The teachings of an ancient Chinese sage.

"In daily life there may be four temptations
That devastate your soul if out of hand,
And merit God's explicit firm command
To take control of evil situations.
These danger zones that cause such desolation:
False witness, force, and wealth and sex, expand
(Unless controlled and even if unplanned),
Into an ethical abomination.
Within the Law, there is no ban on sex;
While not *approving* promiscuity,
Duplicity, flirtation or seduction,
The Law admits these matters are complex,
And only draws this line: *adultery,*
For here the family can face destruction."

"The family is sacred, civilized
Society requires stability;
The passions roused by one's adultery
Reverberate, however ill-advised.
Unfaithfulness, no matter how disguised
Is not compatible with constancy;
The Lord requires a steadfast family
As key into the life He authorized.
The bond of marriage is permanent
And must not be disturbed without just cause;
A married person who gives way to lust
And is the agent of abandonment,
Defiling one of God's own holy Laws,
Will not find favor with this breach of trust."

"All life is sacred, not just yours alone;
It is allowed to bicker and to fight,
To argue and debate, but to ignite
A killing passion, God will not condone.
To jealousies and hatreds men are prone,
But they must be suppressed, kept out of sight,
Lest vengeance and reprisals come to light;
The seeds of murder never must be sown.
These furies are, in animals, restrained;
If intra-species warfare comes about,
The group destroys itself, proceeds until
They all are gone, the war is self-contained.
This end (for Man), the Lord could do without,
And therefore God's command: 'Thou must not kill'."

"The wealth of all this world is there for all
But must be earned, and yet the aptitude,
Bestowed unequally, may not include
Good fortune, often noted to befall
The ones who show more *chutzpah* or more gall.
The wealthy are industrious and shrewd,
Still, if their plans are cunning, even crude,
The Lord does not begrudge their wherewithal.
He *does* object to pilfering and stealing;
Whatever you may have is yours alone,
But nothing more, and none you have not earned.
Fair play does not admit of double-dealing,
The seeds of animosity are sown
And civilized behavior overturned."

"The mandate of the Lord: 'Thou shalt not steal'
Is not so that a few continue rich
But more stay poor, or that they never switch;
For we must realize this world is real,
And not as we would wish it, an ideal.
The poor are always with us, tell me which
Will stay forever in this dismal niche
And who reverse his interim ordeal?
To steal or cheat the ones who, poor already,
Need all they have builds animosity,
And is not fair within the Law of God.
But likewise *they* must work, forthright and steady;
To steal, to get ahead immorally
Is trampling on the righteous path roughshod."

"In conversation, we exaggerate,
In calculation often one will fudge;
With all good faith we frequently misjudge
And estimations are approximate.
There is no *sin* when you equivocate,
In disagreements one may smear or smudge
An adverse detail, God will not begrudge
These aberrations you originate.
But when you are in court and under oath
As testifier, judge or litigant,
No matter with a stranger or your brother,
The Law prohibits equally to both:
To swear to tell the truth and then recant;
You shall not bear false witness to another."

"The precipice is steep, and near the edge
Temptation to look over is seductive;
One minor slip, the fall becomes destructive,
There is no rescue from the crumbling ledge.
And therefore, God has sent a final pledge
Which, if you pay attention, is instructive;
It may seem negative, but is productive,
Avoiding all that leads to sacrilege.
You must not *covet* things that are not yours,
Such as a wife belonging to your neighbor,
(Nor ox, nor ass, nor house nor anything).
To follow this commandment reassures
The Lord that only by your honest labor
And faithfulness will you be profiting."

"To eat, to drink, to dance are authorized
If these are shared with God by means of prayer;
For all reflect His glory and declare
Your gratitude for life, epitomized
By blessings that you offer, undisguised.
You need not fast nor flagellate nor bear
The sins of other men, nor must you swear
A month of abstinence, or be baptized.
God will not ask you to be celibate
Or live a life of holy poverty,
For all belongs to God and must be prized.
A just and righteous life is adequate
If God receives the credit morally;
But one thing more, you must be circumcised."

Then I considered all that he had said,
The glory of the Lord, and how to live,
The energy and force, affirmative
Instead of fearsome demons and of dread.
I knew myself, and looking far ahead,
Saw faith decline, my life was like a sieve,
And needing God to see and to forgive,
Agreed with him, just *slightly* limited.
There is one God, and next to Him are none,
And I would love Him with my heart and mind,
The very most that anyone could do;
This is a noble thing when it is done.
This was the course to which I was inclined:
To keep the Law, but keep my foreskin, too.

Then his demeanor changed, and somewhat sadly,
Conceding that so far his work had failed,
He said that multitudes behaving badly
Had challenged righteousness (but not prevailed).
"There is a line of prophets that, unbroken,
Has held a key denied to other men,
For it is unto them that God has spoken,
Revealing destined sequences and then
They can by virtue of unequalled power
Extrapolate the future from the past.
So I will say that there will be an hour
When finally a prophet comes, the last;
Then He will make the work of God complete
And render ancient priesthoods obsolete."

I knew that I had listened carefully
And understood as much of what he quoted
As I could penetrate, and yet the key
To what I sought, to what I had devoted
These years of searching, all I had committed
Of innocence, of willingness to learn,
Of honest openness, which had permitted
So many minds to teach, and I to earn
The understanding I had gained so far
Eluded me; my insight incomplete,
My comprehension was irregular,
And all my education bittersweet.
For what I knew was still not on a par
With Love, the morning and the evening star.

End of Part III of "*Sacred Verses*"